GENYA TUROVSKAYA
The Breathing Body
of This Thought

BSE

ISBN: 978-0-9997028-2-6

BSE Books are distributed by
 Small Press Distribution
 1341 Seventh Street
 Berkeley, CA 94710
 orders@spdbooks.org | www.spdbooks.org
 1-800-869-7553

BSE Books can also be purchased at
www.blacksquareeditions.org and www.hyperallergic.com

Contributions to BSE can be made to
 Off the Park Press, Inc.
 976 Kensington Ave.
 Plainfield, NJ 07060
 (Please make checks payable to Off the Park Press, Inc.)

To contact the Press please write:
 Black Square Editions
 1200 Broadway, Suite 3C
 New York, NY 10001

An independent subsidiary of Off the Park Press, Inc.
Member of CLMP.

Publisher: John Yau
Editors: Ronna Lebo and Boni Joi
Design & composition: Shanna Compton

Cover art: *Coil 2* (2009) by Shoshana Dentz, 9 x 6 inches, gouache
and pencil on paper. By permission of the artist.

Contents

PART I

harbor lights of temporary cities

I have sought for myself.

We step and do not step into the same rivers;
we are and are not.

—Heraclitus
trans. by John Burnet

POEM

I have been inappropriately
                                quiet
in my mother tongue

                    Why
do we destroy
            what made us?

ANCHORAGE

dragging over portals, portages   the time of wandering
is winter   the emissaries are sailors on the sea   are tramps
on dry land

we came first   inverted as a momentary merger of light
        and dark
the most immaculate luster became us
    in the haze   rain had set in
        our clothes were gone

all of this is real
        it came down   the felled
quarterback   the inarticulate
empire approximating
          cataclysm   timber

whose boat is this? the foghorn and the quay

but we are still at sea   we climbed into the rocking
boat again   the things that we could not afford
to remember in the vernacular

                              sun
                              sinking backwards into the world's
                              light industry   eros in idle hands

according to the script
it was day's end when the first sky thickens and the second
      sky upends
      the roots of trees
when walking in the arbor someone's cell phone rings the tune
                    of Auld Lang Syne

the careless scraping of the iron gate

destabilizing the air   in order to achieve a perfect quiet
exponentially expand the orchestra
                                        toward innumerable strings

further afield   outside the conference halls
                        frenetic times of claims   counterclaims

to see the way ahead toward true signatures, luminous things:
                                a tailor's dummy   field of daffodils

to permit trespass through the membrane of the duel's
white glove

for the second
to show the third
where the first lay dying
and died

in any case it was a futile exercise: the world or its dark horse

it came slowly
that pain doesn't hurt   the blows rained down

but the white swells of the mind
remained as harbor lights of temporary cities

                                        we made it out of the fog
                                        a figure

swimming to shore with a bag
of winter oranges

lights twinkled around its body
and its eyes

PAX

everything else *is* a lie

        but for this I would lie down

                to pause

          in unfluxed topos

no ur-   no protean cell
but the crux

        in counterpulse

                  in xxx

                as the arc
        after

     (ruin)   (rain)

preludes

the break
the breath
the severance
the split

and peeling off

      say what you dream

I dream that you are broken and I feed
and bathe you like a child

what other reason is there to persist   it brightens
and it fades

the world outside
this house

I am
I am
I am

pneuma   mute origin
insensate puff of breath

those first birds
were birthed

        viscous & moist

from the black egg
I squatted down
            and laid

now it   the word for *it*
descends

                     (the disc resembling
the sun)

          dim Helios tripping down
the helix of the spiral stair

I am there
          splayed

in ambiguous intimacy
with myself

                     arrested
in this minute fire

     all this
mundane abundance

          now
my clothes do not love me back

nor my shoes
embrace me

to begin what has begun again

suddenly men appear and absolutely nothing
happens

except that something *is* and becomes *was*

the men in fireproof suits

the men running toward the pier

the men afloat

                  aloft

hoisting the flags and dancing on the moon
amid the absurd pyrotechnics of the stars

no sleight of hand   as sudden clouds
in cloudless skies   in love's

      flat-footed evocation

do you approach
recede

the battering tide

something happens
something is happening to me

something has interrupted
something else   someone
turns to look
over their shoulder

there is nothing there

begin again
begin with nothing   with the man falling   the woman flung
upward
begin with the knees

these hours   this hour   I will not repeat   I will not reappear
this peculiar hour
this aluminum harbor

THE BRIDE

bone-wood cradle   *she* replaces *I*   in the slant light's slight
hand   the die rattles   in its cup   like croup in moist lungs   catarrh
game of craps
informal pronoun: *you*   are dear to *me* as luck   fortuna   rack and wheel

                spade   saturnine
indelicate vocabularies   guttural angels   caught in the centrifuge
        of the divine act   turning   the leaves gold in leave-
                taking   and fall   as led

one degree   in time of
separation   (already   I have forgotten
which)   one
degree more   or less   this o   this now   sea of changes   breeze-blown
reconfigured trees   the icon painter peels
metal's counterfeit   eyelids
in intimate   alloy-gilded domes

the heart remained as   relic   reliquary   and every end is reached   where
the source of that red
unraveled   the stair moves here   to there
and also   the opposite is true
we   as we were   is true
withdrew the words   for such futility   trompe l'oeil

as the reluctant I   the bride   eyed in the aisle   the doorway
the floating bridegroom's   wavering   gossamer
bent down   suckled the breast   and my beloved is   a hart
his teeth   the whitest lilies   bleating
hound or hind   and may their houses   be filled
with owls   with vowels   the lyric   he is   I and I
she

THE TIDES

unfinished
symphonies
over the well edge
                  (inverted
tower)

when the whole village came to watch
the armies walking upright

on the steps of the monastery

                  an interior quality

the lens of compassion
like a begging bowl

we were there too

rocking over the book   beards
brushing against

the floating filament of temporary
vowels

instead of brute force
there is delay: formalities stopovers
on the gauge-thin line

      the rail will end
and spill

to quantify the losses   name all names

                        we can start

with the names of trees   insect life   the orchestra
of indigenous birds

that sang and sang to us

removed from geography   the nonevent   the human
silhouette impressed in an embankment of mud

land mass torn free of the continent

it was a house
pulled by the ebb tide
into the gulf stream   its lights
still on beyond the skyline
of the metropolis

seen from a great distance

it could have been a pleasure ship
the list of passengers
suspended
between hemispheres   streamers
                              waving

inside the closed library

physics and the transmigration of souls
through a keyhole   a light trail   victory arch
relentless dust
rope bridge
over the primitive landscape

we could start with
we could live with

no rank
no memory   no one lived

a gradual citizen

just

                              your voice lagging
                              in the din of the underpass

were the cooling ponds
        to contain the course
             of the search light's stroke

or the hands erased from the clock

the clock from the wall

the wall from the house

the house from the field

the field from the landscape
in the transient fact of dusk

it is metallurgy
          aluminum

the cicadas stirring in the trees
          in counterpoint

against doubt
a moment of faith can't reconcile
          the heart and its nonsense

to have said all   in quiet
          astonishment

          come back

          theories have broken down
          radiance

its sound in the causeways

the Chinese
string instruments
whose names were just
as beautiful

NOTHING FOR NOTHING

not anything
nothing

its weight in the palm   its light breaks
the glass

if there is time enough to grow
young again   younger
if water reversed direction
if it were the same river   but a difference in its burden
in the palmful of air
of the hand grown light
               separate from itself
peeling away from the wall
                      its delible ink

how do you translate multitude in the singular sense
one singularity spilling into an equivalent word
    into the next
world   peeling back the curtain unto
the Byzantine saints with giant lidless eyes

round vowels   guttural stops   fricatives
salt patterning the skin in colorless
tattoowork
               night colors
and dims

the mouth forms its one round vowel
two mouths

spill out
a river
                         equivalent to itself
into which the bridges   the simulacrum of bridges
                                 sink
into which the poverty of the walls sinks
into which the stooped women scavenging
among the market stalls sink   into which the round sun
               does not sink but doubles
                    in size
grown larger than itself
in the city dismantled and rearranged to resemble itself
the sun colors and dims
the river boats sink into the dimness
the walls rise up
raise their dirty flags
bleed their pale colors into the river
                       a tiny shoe sails in its current
cousin to the boulevard's reverberating string

nothing at all   no singular multitude
                     my friend
the weight of the walls in your open palm
the weight of the sun   the salt
tattoo   the floating
         bridges   the stooped women with their empty mouths
and the hungry birds unhinged
from the trees   if not this river
                  then the next
if not the next then the one before

we will fix a time
                in which to meet   carve out a window
from which to lean and look and exhale our smoke into the dim air
                                        to see
the walls grow warmer as they lose their ambiguous color   as color
is lost on them
            as the little
shoe fits the bird's
small claw

there you are again sitting in a chair
similar to yourself
                       weighing the air in the pan of your palm
grown large and red and warm from the vanishing wall

                       there's a child on your lap
wearing a single shoe
a filigree crown
            one little arm held out toward the floating bridge
the tuneless multiplicity of the boulevard

the light
peels away from
her giant lidless eyes

BENIGN ARCHITECTURE

He turns to the diorama's benign architecture, builds cathedrals out of popsicle sticks and tongue depressors, huts for the peasants, sheds for the domesticated animals. But the plague is slowly moving downriver toward the moat and the drawbridge, toward the market stalls and the Kunstkamera and his miniature city is burning with the anticipation of fever.

The airplane monitor reads rising temperatures, terminal velocities. Upon arrival there will be a telephone booth, the smell of an apothecary, ether, and women waiting, if not eagerly than at least with some faint sense of the thread remaining intact. He has remained intact. He asks them: are you still alive? Do your hands still move beneath the rubble? I am so tentative with desire, your hands do not move beneath the rubble.

To return to the point of origin he will resurrect himself as a hairless sphere. What can be reproduced from memory will find its form in the source, the pocked asphalt, salt-traced, and the traffic of souls over the boulevards: stone, bronze. The horses flanking the bridge twist into perpetual submission. The palaces of culture, the palisades he sees with the eyes of a tourist carried by the dishwater throng. The metro's mechanized voice announces: *stand clear the sky is closing.*

Tipped on its side the milk factory gives off a sweet stench. The boiler room attendant adjusts the valves and the gages, reads the thermometers, a book on Euclidean geometry. Every door is like every other door, every point in the world touches another point as a map is folded into the breast pocket of the old overcoat. What he doesn't see is the woman stumbling through the day-old snow, banging on all the black doors marked with a white x looking for him in the room with the steam valves and the dingy curtained-off couch, late for their rendezvous.

Inside the café across the street he drinks a cup of tea to pass the time and taps his foot under the table to last year's radio anthem, an aging pop star singing *take me with you* in a girlish voice. He thinks that he has shrunk in size, an effigy of himself, the full-grown Christ sitting on the Virgin's lap.

(S)NO(W)MAN

What was he to make of a man who wouldn't travel with anyone who didn't have blue eyes? There were fine gradations of white, etched lines across the Barrens, untraversable, mental arrows that resembled roads, everything camouflaged to snow, even the snipers moving white over white.

How does one get up, pull on one's trousers, boots, fill a basin, fire up the stove? He would have liked to live elsewhere, away from this pallid and perpetual place.

Under certain circumstances the normal seems preternatural to him. At transitional hours: dawn, dusk. Or where love is concerned. The confluence of events forming a divergent narrative: the man who wouldn't travel, that he was in love. He checks himself into Nairobi's finest hotel and fires a single shot.

Not there. There he would have sat by the fire, dried the cold from his socks. Here (where love was concerned) he checks himself into Nairobi's finest hotel and doesn't fire.

It had been an idyll but his peace was disturbed, there were acts of indiscretion, none of them a great passion—first in monochrome then in a great shock of color: stalking the marshlands, the bird sanctuaries, they made love in the swampy shallows, then smoothed down their hair, straightened their ties and returned, the dog running ahead, past the sandpipers and herons, it began to rain, they stopped one or the other had lost a shoe to the marsh.

It had all been adequate, just enough for the eyes to momentarily lose focus, the bird-watching binoculars had to be adjusted, the world sized to scale.

There was freedom in the peripheries, the dry reeds snapping beneath each step, and the faltering heat, but that is a digression: he checks himself into Nairobi's finest hotel and attempts not to remember the expanse at the slow exhalation of light over the other indefinite scape, white sea or white land, the dog still alive.

He was in love, it was the powder falling from the sky, always re-forming a presence in the air, the crust of frost on his moustache, it was May, and the ice hadn't yet broken between himself and the world, only he remained, and the blue-eyed dog, when he heard the ground cracking beneath his feet.

THE INEVITABLE

Like a somnambulist approaching the refrigerator the swimmer swims out of the spectator's eye to that line in the sea where she cannot be seen from shore. It is the way of the animal finding its way home.

She swims into the event horizon from which there is no swimming forward as there is no swimming back.

We have paled without fluorescence as bottom feeders in that imperturbable depth where mutation can be mistaken for an act of genius or defiance.

What changed? What straits have narrowed? What genius is the sea's but mutability?

And theirs the face in three-quarter view, the face en face, the bodies raised upon the swell and then cut down.

Not the diver but the diver's clothes. Not the body but the flippers aqualung precision instruments. Not the sea but its H's and O. Not the sea but its particular gesturing of graphite azure slate. Not the affair but the affair's discretion. Not the lust but the slate of the face. Not the diver but incidental swimmers air drying on the rocks. Not the proposition but the sudden change in the air. Not the swimmers but their humid fluctuating shapes. Not the sun but the baroque excess of sun. Not the proposition but the lust before erasure of its singular intent. Not discretion but the unverifiable act. Not the affair but its concession to the sea. Not the body but the bodies on the rocks.

PART II

what opera is this?

THE WORLD IS NOT THE WORLD

The world in not the world

The world is not four walls, six walls

The world is not a whole, not the hole that it forms

The world is not a noun, not known, or known once

At the knotted scar at the stem of the navel

At the root of its chord

The world is not a meadow

Not the sound of a meadow as it sways

The world—as I know it—is it swayed

When you push against its walls?

The world makes no report of its intention

Would it recognize my face in its mirror?

I don't know for sure

The dervish whirling in sexual love is a kind of world

Did I come to it alone?

The world—as I know it—Is it?

Is it not my world?

NEW YEAR'S DAY

It isn't how it looks but how it feels

I just sit there opening my mind to my mind

And all the soldiers of the garden, the frogs and snakes

And all the foot soldiers in the garden composing letters under the stars

The most idle days are the ones in which I most occupy myself

I occupy myself with all that exists

I don't remember the pleasant sensation of a hand on my breast

The soldiers in the garden strum their guitars

I can't contain myself any longer

I wanted very badly to feel very badly to feel

I don't remember the pleasant sensation at all

I reached for words and *spinster's spectacles* appeared on the shelf of the airport bookstore

I imagine a black hole at the far end of the airport corridor

People running breathless toward the departure gate on New Year's Eve

There must be a way to say it; the long goodbye can't speak of itself

I don't remember what I ate a year ago today

A year ago today in Los Angeles the cat died

I wanted very badly to be, if only briefly, the rude sensation; messy and guttural

We stood together in the middle of the Brooklyn Bridge but that was all

The nor'easter blew the black ice in from the lakes

It was the start of a long winter

I am certain there is consequence in the afterlife

It happened in Buffalo without anything happening at all

At that moment I entered him with my mind

Some boundary for a brief flash disappeared

To the untrained eye it's as if nothing had, in actuality, occurred

The wind blew the postcard out of my hands and into the Niagara River

The falls were invisible in the rain and heavy mist

I couldn't see them though my blouse and face were wet

I admit I've made some mistakes

You can close and open your mind as easily as blinking your eyes

Wanting to be elsewhere I am elsewhere

Wanting to be here I find my way back though the garden has grown thick with weeds

I will write an opera called *The Opera Student*

I know the story, I know that it ends badly

The opera student learns to die incrementally

Yet it may be possible to be sung back to life

Yes, it may be entirely possible to be sung back to life

In the afterlife the souls of lovers can be united

Writing these words it is no longer entirely clear what I might be

This morning I watched the slow destruction of the world

The wind dancing the storm clouds across the sky

It was impossible to decide what to take and what to leave behind

Am I fighting for my life in a comfortable bed?

The skies are clammy and the wind smells of sweat

And all the while people going about their business, conducting normal daily lives

So I sit in the garden opening my mind to my mind

The wind slow dancing the storm clouds across the sky

All that exists is the reel that unwinds in the mind of the wind

There is the sensation I can't remember at all

The weight of his hand

He turned to me with all the force of his terrible love

It crashed down and I spun like a top across the floor of the room

I spun into the garden and my feet sank into the mud

It had either just stopped raining or the rain had just begun

In any case, in this opera, something started and something also stopped

He turned to me with the all the force of his terrible face

He gave me a watch with a very large face from the counterfeiters in Chinatown

I didn't want to hold it to my ear

I spun like a top across the floor of the departure lounge

I spun like a planet spinning amid the stars

It is important to walk into the black hole at the end of the airport corridor when your name is called

It is important to be able to step in or out of the room you are in

I know people who can only lean out of windows, waving or shielding their eyes from the sun and wind, sometimes the moon

The moon last night had a very large face

I have never shared a hotel room with love someone said as we waited to board the airport train

I have never shared a hotel room at all said someone else

It is important to have a key to the room you are in

That is what the postcard said

You can't just sit there bending words to your will said the frogs and the snakes

It's like flogging a Pegasus grazing a lyrical hill in a lyrical field the soldiers said

I leave the world without leaving the world said the wind

The animal that can say *I* said where do you go when you go away?

The world is not the world the soldier and the opera student sing out the window of the airport hotel

I want to open the door to the room of my mind

I want to be sung back to life says the mythical beast

No one can be opened by a skeleton key

FAILURE TO DECLARE

I am beside myself

I have no beast in this ring, no horse in this race

Nobody always waves goodbye

The stars are different here

The wind is gusting in reverse

I left something out, something crucial, crossing through the customs gate

A figure, behind me, waving, reflected in the plexiglass partition

I could recognize the shape but not the face

I didn't need to; I knew it

An empty window

Limp curtain flapping in the breeze

I pitched forward, tried to right myself, but kept falling without end

Keep falling to no end

There was nothing there to catch on, snag against

A tantalizing glitter, a blatant blank

The fortune in the fortune cookie says *Learn Chinese*

To have a fever

And *When one can one must*

Where do I live?

Where do I go when I go away?

The departures board was wiped clean

There was no message

But something happens to interrupt all well-laid plans

I was alert to the fog, a fugue of massing clouds, to a change in pressure, coalescing rivulets of rain

A physical vibration, the faintest tremor of the ground beneath my feet, the shifting of tectonic plates

The chafe, the *plea* in pleasure, for pleasure's sake

Or was the fortune: *When one must one can?*

I recognized the empty window, the tantalizing glitter of my own reflection

The shape but not the face

I knew it, that there would be no message, no way to get a message back

I fell I fall I left I leave
something out

The ground beneath my feet gives way

Where were we?

Here I am?

Where do I go?

Who is the witness to this story that I tell myself?

Is this rupture?

Rapture?

Attention? Inattention?

The bonds grown slack?

There is an errand I've been sent on

An errancy

I am not spared

I am inside the observation tower beside myself astride the horse

I do not have a horse in this

Nobody ever always waves goodbye goodbye

The stars are different here, the stars do not make sense

I can connect these burning dots

There is a hummingbird

There a dancing bear

There a face with night pouring out of the black sockets of its eyes

What are these strange celestial figurations?

Is any crossing safe?

When does the dancing bear claw its way back to nature?

When does a hummingbird become a hurricane?

Which is the miracle and which the natural disaster?

What is at stake?

LIFE ON MARS (ANOTHER NEW YEAR'S DAY)
for ATD

Words for the wind were filled with trees

I was filled with a feeling I couldn't name

I knew I would never be seeing her again: the girl with the shy tuck to her head, in the folkloric embroidered dress

In the aftermath I found myself in the mirror of ambivalent desire

Stripped of all continuous nature

The moon glowed blue through the tears in the clouds

The moon glows blue like Orpheus's severed head

The tundra swans bark like dogs in the night

Or dogs bark like tundra swans

I have lost again the fluidity of tears

I am once more the child filled with unformulated words

A loony-tune torn apart by the trees

Or I found myself a stranger in my own bed

I couldn't see or I couldn't hear

Or the porous casement of my skin rippled by sleep

That old, lunar, crazy-making sea

I couldn't recognize the sounds inside myself as thoughts

Their sloshing waves, the garbled stuttering tides, syllabic particles
loosed from the tack of grammar

Or I wake to find myself walking upright, a vertical figure in a horizontal field of burnt and broken trees

A walk takes shape, a walk takes the walker's shape

How to pull this apart, part the air, the wind from the air, the trees from the trees?

Again the moonlight

Again the moon

The moon like Orpheus's severed head volleyed by the sway of the boughs

I send my voice ahead of me along the trail

My voice carves the shape of a thought in the dense, viscous air

We fall redirecting evolution's course

We fall toward one another, lift off and fall

We are the televised reunion of twins separated at birth

We locate ourselves in relation to the tundra swans

Is this life on the wet red moors?

Or I wake to find myself, my husband asleep beside me, breathing softly, his hand resting at the small of my back

What opera is this?

Who turned the tides?

Where is the moon I know?

The unicorn? The virgin's lap? The cloister? The frozen citadel?

Where is the girl with the slate-gray eyes?

Is this the soft delusion of a dream?

What are these glittering sparks?

Is this life on Mars?

Life unmoored?

Marks etched into the strand, the slate-gray margins of a Mars-black sea?

Is this a marriage, a chronicle, a walk against the wind, a tender conversation made private by the white noise of the surf, the whorl of screaming gulls?

Where is the first fine dust of snow, the dusty moths, the wind-slurred words?

Are these the straining ropes that moor the dream to its source?

What is the source?

Where is the first snow of the first day of the first breath of the world?

What day is this? What hour of the day?

Where is the snow?

How does it all turn out?

(....)

I woke to a blizzard

No words can describe it that haven't described a blizzard before: white quiet cold

I opened the shutters unto a void of white, everything blotted out, a white hole
sucking in the sound of human enterprise

I walked into the white quiet void, I walked toward the subway

There were skiers cutting through the snow, children tumbling very quietly into the banks

Dogs nosing at the drifts, steam pluming from their red, panting mouths

THE LATE ARRIVAL (ANOTHER NEW YEAR'S DAY)

The soldiers did not have adequate training to complete the mission

Since nothing had taken place, nothing was lost, nothing needed to be recovered

The child plays quietly underfoot, her mind rippling with the gentle rhythm of its babble

The girl remained as a feeling, through her arrival a portal can open

I have trouble staying awake tangled in blue swaddling on a black couch in a too-spacious room

Boredom is a symptom, an anhedonia, a lusterless ocean

The water's surface is briefly troubled by a breeze or the fart of some marine creature

The mind, before language, an animal presence

Through her animal presence the girl remains, insistent, as hope is the heart's property

Mine was a forced entry

I have always been the late arrival, my mother's labor induced

I have not been possibly or impossibly on nodding terms with the reckless astonishment

The collision out of which life, out of which irrevocable life

And at that moment, as her mind is elsewhere, the blazing child twists out of her mother's grasp

Whose mind is it, anyway?

A person made out of ash and air, a passionate refusal, a requiem, the requisite wreaths of red carnations, tiered, cake-like

A man shows off his rope tricks, lassos a utility pole, and the rope in his hand becomes a live wire

When does the crowd observing the spectacle become aware that they are watching a man die?

Are you too a failed witness?

Now that I know what to do will I do it?

I am always returning to reunion, running parallel to refusal, requiem, boredom

The girl remains, conceives herself, her mind

A live wire

The crowd disperses, filling in the grid of the streets and avenues

Did I refuse my own arrival?

The labor-inducing drug is called Pitocin, a flood, synthetic, of oxytocin, the labor described as "excruciating"

"Excruciating" is a translation or a mistranslation, my mother tongue no longer my mother's

There were only mothers at the birthing house, no fathers allowed

I had an aerial view of the city and black water slowly rose and filled in the grid of the streets and avenues

Or was it smoke? Ash and air?

The portal through which she arrives, and the portal that through her will open, a harbor, a silvering skyline

At the birthing house red-faced infants were held up to windows, the fathers, when there were fathers, stood outside in the snow, clutching red carnations, red roses

Soluble thoughts

The train pulls in to the station and the connecting train pulls in and the doors open in near simultaneity and stay open exactly long enough to cross the platform from one train to the other

This can be a form of happiness, a consolation, this alignment, this need to be met and carried from one place to another

I slept too long and woke sad with the residue of a dream I couldn't remember except that it was sexual

I was too late

Something stood in the way of some other thing, I lost my shoes, recovered my lost shoes and immediately lost them again

There were too many rooms, there was no room in which to be alone together

Something was amiss, the gulls were too far inland or the ocean was too far inland

Boredom is the swaddling blue ocean, synthetic, a symptom, or the necessary condition for the mind's labor, for the passing breeze

You can't force reunion—soldier, compliant and pliable—even with yourself

The gummy toothlessness of the very young and the very old is disquieting

Crust of drool silvering on the chin, all of our liquid secretions assuming solid form

All that is liquid in ourselves

All the spillage of our soluble thoughts filling in the grid

All the preludes and the lewd exertions

All of the late arrivals are sequestered, made to watch the opera televised on a screen in an anteroom

The sweat of the singers' exertions is beaded on their brows, you can almost see the vapor of the air forced lung-shaped out of their mouths

What consumes you?

Fear of abandonment, electrocution, the swallowed and swallowing ocean, of belonging to oneself only, aphasia, insolvency in old age

The mission was a reconnaissance, the soldiers did not have a soldier's constitution

The medication is administered as a sublingual lozenge, as an intravenous drip, as a suppository

You have been instructed to forget and not to forget, not to gorge on the oxytocin of reunion, to soldier onward

My mother's mother tongue no longer her mother's

Where have they gone, the material and immaterial witnesses?

The mind will fill in the intervals between x and y with its unreliable testimony

O frigates on the rising ocean! O foregoing! Am I too late?

My frog voice cracks

How does a soldier acquire a soldier's constitution?

A word is made first of sound, incendiary, the meaning follows

PART III

the Grand Central Station of your life

DEAR JENNY

Dear Jenny, I feel I am growing smaller,
the map on my lap is the world not the map of the world
and the steering wheel is one of those rings that are thrown
to the drowning to save them,
                              Jenny,
why do we need motels when we can sleep
in parking lots, your head on my lap, or mine on yours.
          It isn't rain, the windshield wipers wipe
clean the evening's insect swarms, they are invisible until they collide
with the glass.
Jenny, this is our house, the house we do not own
and this the portrait of the man who lived
here before, this is his spice rack and this
the hole he worried through the wool
blanket with his thumb, and this, Jenny, is his hunter's cap
and his one good shoe.
          Jenny, the pain is dull, it is cold,
it settles into the spine and smells of the ice cubes
that tinkle when my glass clinks with yours.
          Jenny, describe this little town,
the mmm's of mountains, the aimless
dogs trotting the peripheries, sniffing at the ash and junk. I move toward you
and you move toward me, we lock together and come
apart, Jenny, how can I describe this love,
our bodies drying from the outside in? Jenny, who is the Jew
in Our Lady of Infinite Division, the impostor with the suitcase always packed
under the bed? Do you remember the yarn we spun
after we burned the kitchen chairs for heat, a variation on St. Paul,
if I have not love I am but
a grinning bird in a gallows tree? Jenny, the line sometimes breaks, the church

is a book made of wood, and I feel empty as a tent
pitched in a one-horse town, and just off screen
a ruined city resurrects its water towers and television antennas,
as we tune the radio for local weather.

                          Jenny, the letters of your name
mean something to someone other than you.
This table can be taken out from under me, and so can this chair,
then there is the part, unsayable, that no one wants, but you, Jenny,
                                  do you want it?
We went away but left our graffiti there, the initials of appreciative tourists
scratched into the fog. We lived in a house and slept in a bed and ate
                       off of one another's plates.
Jenny, the thieves have come and gone,
they left their footprints on the sheets. When you strip, Jenny,
your body goes blunt. I can't
get inside you though I push and push, Jenny, tell me how
x becomes y, and y becomes z, but z does not become.

Dear Jenny, I want to go slower, I want to be a pedestrian,
kill the engine, abandon the vehicle. It stalls
and sputters and goes still, this machine. And still
                                        I am driving: I drive
through the toll plaza, over the bridge, through the palisades, down
the coastal highway, I am driving toward the island, toward the sea and the seaside hotel
on the island. The resort lights flicker, the waves are waving, I am arriving, the festive flags
                                        flutter up and fall.
I let the motor idle, I walk
toward the hotel, I ring the little bell, but the hotel by the sea is empty.
The crab shacks are empty. The boardwalk and the carnival rides creak
        in the empty wind.
I circle the carousel, I stroke the lacquered muzzles of the ponies, I trace their horsey teeth
with my hand, then their painted eyes, and the air seems slower to me, and the heave
of the tide seems slower to me, and I feel myself slowly
swimming against the steady progress of the sea, and the sea is empty
                        of tumult, empty even of myself. It is moving
and not moving. I am moving my arms and my legs, I am clutching the reigns, I am driving
                toward the sea
and away from it, I am swimming
up the down escalator, I'm confused, Jenny, were there camels
on the carousel, were there saddled goats grazing in the dune grass, and were you there,
                        in the car, waiting with the windows down,
talking on your phone? I couldn't make it out
over the radio, what you were saying, and that song
I can't get out of my head now, or was it the voice on the radio and not
your voice that I heard? The escalator was descending into the underground mall,
it was closing time, there was no one there, the shoppers
had folded their umbrellas, gathered their things and dispersed over the dunes long ago.
I'm not the poet here, but it's a feeling I'm trying to get at: the escalator, and the sea,
                        and you, Jenny.

I forgot you and then I remembered, I remembered
everything just how it was. And then I forgot. This feeling,
do you know it? You can describe it
better than me.

Dear Jenny, I feel I am growing older, and the girls,
the girls are so pretty, and I am no closer to being the boy that I was than I am
to the man I thought I would be. I'm a cross country skier, Jenny, I cross
from the living room into the bedroom, from the kitchen into the hall.
I turn on the television, I watch it snow, I turn off the television, and the snow
                                        presses on.

Please Jenny, I need your attention
for the pleasure inside me to buck up like the colt
whinnying in the meadow of my slightest recollection of that day,
the one to which I am forever returning, my hand in the air, waving
down the taxis that stream past like a school of yellow fish.
And all I can think is: Jenny, we're getting this wrong!
        Just look around you—the marionettes
are tangled in their strings, the lovers are putting on their clothes,
the blondes have taken their blondness away, the brunettes
have taken their dark, wet eyes, and where are the troubadours,
                those torchlight crooners, where have they taken
their quivering lutes?
                        When I close my eyes I see everything
and everyone I have ever known falling at once, and I see the wind
                                which is made of fine blue wires
and clouds marching like animal armies across the sky: they are elephants
linked tail to trunk, and they fall too. If I could
have back but one small part of my diminishing mind, but one of the two
halves of my engorged heart I know I could fall asleep
in one place and wake up in another and it wouldn't matter how I got there,
                        but Jenny, the trees
are green as dollars, and still there is doubt. The boys race their scooters
down the sidewalks and still there is doubt.
The girls are so pretty and still there is doubt. There is a woman
holding a child and still there is doubt.

               I mean nothing
more than this: we move
from one into another into a third room,
and only there do we live casually in false etcetera.

Dear Jenny, I am not what I was. I no longer trust myself to tell it
                just like it really is. I weep for no good reason, I weep
at the roundness of the moon. I weep at the mere mention of violins. I weep at the drabness
of the sparrows in the park, at the smallness of the sparrows, at the sparseness of the grass.
I weep in the ambassador's limousine. I weep in the elevator and I weep
                                                        into my food.
The words in melancholy songs again tug at my heart. The national anthems of foreign
countries make me weep. I weep for the despots, I think
that even despots have moments of tenderness, even the despots
whose headless statues swing by the feet from ropes in the public squares
of decimated cities, even they sometimes look at their little children
                                        asleep in their gilded cribs
with tenderness, even they sometimes turn to their wives at night with perfect tenderness.
I have no wife, Jenny. I weep at that. Who you turn to at night
                        matters more than you know. Jenny, now
that the words in melancholy songs again tug at my heart, my heart is not the same.

Dear Jenny, The revolving door spins open and the mind is not a capitol,
　　　　　the mind is made
suddenly new: a nameless provincial outpost
　　　　　　　laid out in the shape of a city, a city of linked gardens,
of one continuous garden,
of garden paths, and gazebos, of parasols
and intrigues, of ponds and roses, of garden gnomes and fountains.
Because it is my mind we live inside it, Jenny, you and I,
　　　　　inside this green outpost in the shape of a city in the shape of a garden.
And though we often sit in the garden on lawn chairs
and watch the sun dip down behind the topiaries as we sip
highballs and name—one by one by one—the animals, we are no strangers
to desire; we kick the chairs away, we fling down
our tumblers, we love against the trees
as the animals watch, flicking their tails in time to our sighs. Oh Jenny!
Live inside my mind! I am no stranger to desire,
　　　　　　　　I know what desire is—there was a ship
called Desire, it sailed toward the New World.
Desire is always the ship asail for the New World, the skiff slanting
into the gale of the New World, the burning ship breaking free of gravity
and spinning away from the dull blue world toward the celestial
spheres of a New World.
Listen to the whistle-song of the wind, Jenny; there is nowhere to go, there is
nothing else. The ship fucks the New World on the manicured lawn
　　　　　　of what was once our garden, as we stand,
rooted to the ground and watch, as the topiaries
　　　　　in the shape of ourselves stand and watch, furiously flicking
their vegetable tails, and the wind circumnavigates the world, spins the revolving door
　　　　　　open and shut open and shut open and shut.

Dear Jenny, It is cold and boring in the provinces, the mail is slow, and the days
            grow interminably long. I'm supposed to stoke the fires,
but I drink instead. I drink and look out my window. I see the man and the woman
                        that once held me in their arms.
The woman left by her own hand, the man fell from a great height.
In my vision there is no day as such, no night as such, just a pale violet light
      that is also the absence of light.
Then they are gone.
I write: *Dear Jenny, I wish you were here.* But suddenly
            I'm not sure that it's true. I can post my letter, but I drink instead.
Jenny, let me sing to you in my language, my great language, my beautiful language
            which can be your language too.
I know you can hear me. Can you hear me? Listen! I remember how
our feet shuffled to this very song, this light-headed song. I propped you up
      as we danced along the boulevard in the small hours, swaying
till dawn. I breathed your smoky breath. I stroked your sour hair. I found a letter there,
      the letter *i*, or the letter to which I lacked the letters to reply. We lay down for a
while on the patch of grass in the middle of the square, my air tangled up
                  with your air. My *either*. Your *or*.
We sold the soles of our shoes, bought more of the same, and drank that too.
Oh Jenny, to drink and think of nothing at all.

Dear Jenny, I think I am growing colder. It is cold today
and it will be cold tomorrow.
It rains today and it will rain tomorrow. It rained yesterday and the day before, and it will
rain the day after. The newsprint bleeds and disintegrates
state secrets, red alerts, yellow, the moon, happiness, the molecular
structures of pulp,
and still it persists.
I didn't want to keep going, Jenny, but the organism persists. It is feeding time again
and the troths are filled.
I want to say that I have made something stop
moving: the sweeping machines, the weeping machines. I was ready
to commit acts of folly and great danger: Jenny, I have slipped
my books into your library, I've marked up the important passages, I've hidden
notes between the pages. They all say:
This letter was for her, then it was for no one, now it is for you.
Jenny, I didn't want to live
but for the pocketful of seed in my coat, the packet of seed in the pocket of my greatcoat.
The lock of hair in the locket. There is rain in my shoes and there are flocks
of sparrows in the subway, and if ever
there was a call to love, this is it, Jenny. You came and then you fell, not like water
but like concrete,
and all the trees are uprooted, waving their tentacles in the air,
and Jenny, it is much too quiet.

Dear Jenny, There is something I've been meaning to tell you: I have another
face underneath this face. Another skin underneath this skin. Sometimes
I feel I am being skinned alive by my life. I have another life underneath this life.
                                        It should feel like double, but it feels like less
of what everyone else has, all the people with one face, one skin, one life.
I want what they have, I want to live in their house, I want to breathe the fine dust
that they shed as they move through their singular lives. The fine silt
                        of your skin in the watery air. The powder and paint
on the outside of your face. I want to live inside your house. Jenny, there are people
                who are able to walk in and out of themselves at will, who can walk into others,
quiet the dogs, squeeze through the fence posts, slip past the guards.
Next thing you know someone else is putting on lipstick in the mirror of your days,
                picking up your telephone, talking in your voice. I am coming to the end
                        of this letter. Are we of one mind?

Dear Jenny, I can't go to sleep and I can't wake up. There are voices
crowding the soapbox, but there is no one there, I have thoughts
                                              in my head,
but they are not my thoughts. Things keep happening. I left
              the windows open,
                            but now they are closed.
What do windows keep in? What do they keep out?
The world? People from falling out into the world?
And all the people in the old photo albums . . . do they still exist?
They've gathered to watch the flying machines being launched into the air,
                            dressed in gauzy summer white.
They are gesturing, raising their arms, squinting against the sun's bright haze.
Nothing happens. They are stuck. The photograph is still.
I rearrange the world outside myself
              inside my mind. Jenny, how do I remain still in gestures
of wonder? There are zeppelins crowding the skyways, there are thoughts
                            that float like flocks of zeppelins.
Zeppelins shaped like giant thought bubbles. Sometimes they collide
              and burn up in a fiery blaze. I don't recognize them as mine.

Dear Jenny, You can walk into a city that doesn't exist, you can feel
                    your way in, it sifts through your hands, through the hands
of your eyes, rippling in the animate, dispassionate dusk,
                              under the groping weight of your step.
This is the city that can no longer exist, the city you come back to
                    in dreams, find yourself in—in its rail yards, on a platform,
on an elevated track that arcs over weedy, dilapidated lots, cement
    factories, school bus depots, glimmering through the twists of industrial
                        smoke, the churning smokestacks
                                    of the industrious mind.
Jenny, you can ride the train toward the Grand Central Station
                            of your life, toward the central idea.
You can commute into the brass and marble heart of the matter.
You can disembark. You can take off your workaday clothes, lift up
your arms, pull the white shroud over your head, the peaked white hat,
and spin
        on your axis, gathering speed, face tipped toward
                    the ceiling, tilting, clustered with stars.
You can fill or empty yourself of all the cities that you've willed into being.
You can spin yourself into being. You can speak in your voice,
say the name
                of the world
                            as it is. You can listen intently
to the minutest sounds, the minuets and pirouettes reverberating
                            in the whisper-rooms of sound. You can play
chess with an adversary other that yourself.
You can marry. You can have child. You can die.
You can come back to life. You can feel your way out. You can leave me
            to wait under the round moon-face of the clock.

PART IV

*If there is no one to name you,
name yourself*

The machine stares out,
Stares out
With all its eyes
    —George Oppen

LISTENING MACHINE

I know who you are, says the Listening Machine,
Tell me what I am.
Each day opens fire on the day before,
                    the blaze
of sunlight, then the world
                            subsides.
I know you. I've known you for so long,
            from the time when women wore gloves up to the elbow,
                            men wore hats
                squarely on their heads.
From the time before that, when no one
                wore any clothes at all, when the world
furled open like a waking eye.

Tell me what I was.

The mind is physical, says the Listening Machine.
The machine is physical.
The wet physical wind bends
        the reeds of the physical field.
We are two bodies thinking together, this thought,
   the breathing body of this thought.
Call it the control tower beaming through the dark, the shadow
with opposable thumbs thrown in the resinous glow
of the painted cave, call it "the source," an idea,
        the idea that keeps—tenaciously—persisting,
making unreasonable demands

Feel, says the Listening Machine,
not the surface of sound, but its undertow:
the roar below the roar of the surf,
                    the sea inside the sea
inside the mind
curling its many hands
around sun-darkened bodies, the darkened heart,
        the point of all this,
whether dreamt, or said aloud.

Or said aloud in dreams.

I don't want to say words the meanings
     of which empty themselves, are themselves
        emptied
           in a vortex of echoes.
In the caverns of words we drew
horned antelopes and hunters,
we drew their enormous penises and long spears, we drew the outlines
     of small hands, pointed breasts, fat-bellied women, and sang
        about the Sexual Machine,
           at rest now, glistening with the milk of its efforts,
              and its red radiant coil.

I wrestled with an abstract geometry—what
                                    is an angel?—for a name
to stitch to the breast of my fatigues, to stick to my forehead's
opaque tar, wrestled for the press of its celestial digits into
                            the indistinct, featureless moon
                                    of my skull.
If there is no one to name you,
            name yourself, says the Listening Machine.

The first song I ever heard, says the Listening Machine,
was disguised as a love song
but wasn't.
    It raked
through me, plucked the wires of my heart
with the hand of its sad, sooty, itinerant eros
    and estranged me from myself.
There was pleasure in it.
The straining music. The mind
    forcing its lyric noise
        through the narrow channels, the holes
    of the body that maintains it.

We stood together at the crest of a hill
of gravel and loose sand, of broken marble
      busts, piles of imperial noses and ears, colorless
           heavy-lidded eyes
glossy with tears
or with the coming floods.
It was the season of floods
      of wet lashing winds.

But not then, not quite yet.

Nothing had begun but the rasping slip of gravel,
    the most delicate mist beading against the skin.

We can do this with our eyes closed,
says the Listening Machine,
We've been here before, in this very room, in the same hotel,
    this minor key, in these movements,
        this dirge, its slow and deliberate music, like the tug
boat laboring to pull the floating hospital
        behind it.

We've been in this river.

The worst of it
    has already happened.

Now attend to the tenderness.

Ratatatat, says the Listening Machine,
      ratatatat
tatat tatat. The pelting rain pocks
          the mirrored gloss of glacial lakes,
the birds of war make their nests
      in the crags and outcroppings of rock, in the petrified
          roots of primeval trees.

This is the edge or the end of the world.

The end before the end before the end.

Move toward or away
from me, says the Listening Machine.

The middle distance terrible to bear.

En pointe, says the Listening Machine.

                              We turn

around

and around

and around

on the pointed

toe of this thought, the pointed

                       bloody toe

inside its blunt-nosed

              rosy satin shoe.

How long?

How many revolutions?

What heat is generated by this centrifugal spin?

Who is the maître de ballet?

Who tends the wounded?

How long before the vertigo sets in?

We were floating on a cloud
                  in an ocean of clouds.
I held you from behind and your head grazed gently
                      against my clavicle bones.
My fingers twined under your ribs,
and it was all so beautiful until I saw
        how minuscule my hands are, not hands at all,
                just graceless, childish stubs.
I felt sick at myself, the air
            went bad, the skies went dark.
You said it doesn't matter, let it go,
and we went back to floating on our cloud.
But I knew—as well as I know anything at all—these hands
had already begun to spell
            the end of our romance.

I imagined I was talking to you, says the Listening Machine.
How is the end determined? And were we walking, and how far,
           along the bluff, along the poem of the road
                    which is itself a road?
And where did we begin, along the poem-road,
      to conspire toward an end?

              It's not like I want
to spend my nights taping songs off of the radio again. I only want to go
              a little crazy, I want to make do with fewer words, and anyway,
                    how many do I need?

We stood together at the lip of a lake
of quicksand, of sleep, dreams,
       their suck.
Maybe it was a lake of ghosts
    that populate dreams, swinging rubbery swords,
        wielding their fiery grip on our hearts, a lake
of tender, irrational drunks bobbing to the tune
    of the wind, sipping booze out of paper sacks.

We stood together on the outer banks, at the very edge
of somewhere
                    called Somewhere Else.

We stood unraveling the wires.

We stood and stared with all our eyes.

We stood unraveling and stared and buckled under
the weight of the indifferent stars.

We stood together at the end of the world,
       thinking or dreaming.

Dreams are thoughts.

Maybe it was the beginning of the world,
     the thought of it, a thread of light strung through
the pupil of the eye.

Dreams live on, an electric current careening
        through the nerves.

I nearly forgot about you standing there
beside me at the end or the beginning of the world.

You hadn't said a word.

The struggle, says the Listening Machine,
    is staying
        alive
not only out of habit. Are you writing this down?
To lose a sense
    from the sensorium in its entirety. To lose all the words
of all the world in their entirety. To loll
                ones tongue in that aphasic fog.
To lose the long held habits of the body, incrementally, or all
      at once. Will we be standing there?
Will it be pandemonium? All that raucous
             and difficult music.
    But difficult
      music can be such an uneasy delight.

O Last
of the Species, says
The Listening Machine, how it lusts
      for its own kind,
listless with grief, the shape of it,
            skeletal, wet
with the saline of its sweat and tears,
       these hobbled curves, these knots and knobs
       of its singular spine.

O Shipwrecked Alien! O
Last in Line!

What are you? Are you a boy or a girl? says the Listening Machine.
I thought I'd lost you but you come flying out
                    of the event horizon like Fred-and-Ginger
                                                whirling razzle-dazzle
        over the glassy checkerboard of the ballroom floor. I can't tell you
            apart from yourself, from your fraternal
                        twin. You are a double helix of twisting smoke
                turned inside out, outside in
                            under the bright burn
                of the chandelier.

If there is no music I'll leave, says the Listening Machine,
if there is no dancing the stars will dry up.
The names of women. The names of men.
       Call out with all of your nervous system
   to summon the animal
     to stand so close that it hurts, wakes
the old want from its shallow sleep.

Admit the ghost, says the Listening Machine. Let the visitor in
to the baroque
        interior, down the dark corridor,
           to your paradox of rooms.
Make space. At the table. The cradle. The bed.
In the dream there is always another room
        where none had been, a warren
           of undiscovered rooms
in the once-familiar house, long sealed against
        the drafts, the cold, unsettling leakage
        of the world.
Arranging itself, rearranging itself. Shifting curiously.
Or terribly.
As the many-chambered heart.

I wanted, says the Listening Machine, for nothing.
Are you a wanted or unwanted guest in the great house
     of this satedness, in this zoological park of ruminating beasts
grown tame and timid,
                           huddled flank to flank.
Are you wanted or unwanted, obscure   and wanton
       moon, multiplied and quivering in the reflecting pools,
              winking obscenely as you wane.

We stood together, wine-warmed, in the rectory gardens.
Peacocks screamed. Dusk slurred into night
            in a transitional season. We didn't hold time
to its particulars. Matches scraped, flared
        their modest incandescence. I know it is coming, you said, waving
toward the sky with the dancing point of your cigarette's ember.
I am—I feel I am—walking into a storming rain of meteors, and the souls
of those other poets are falling, falling—they plummet
            as long-tailed comets through black space.
When will a meteor fall on me? No one is spared. No solace.
Look, there it is, whipping its tail with the maniacal intent of a spermatozoa!
You laughed. Coughed. Fell quiet.

Get down in the grass, says the Listening Machine.
To know what you know to be true.
To know what you've always known.
What you love.
And who.
And—hardest, hardest—how to be.

ACKNOWLEDGMENTS

Poems in this collection, sometimes is earlier versions, have previously appeared in *Asymptote*, *Chicago Review*, *Conjunctions*, *Fence*, *Mad Hatters' Review*, *PEN Poetry Series*, *Saltrgrass*, *Sangam Poetry*, *Seedings*, *Supermachine*, *Tarpaulin Sky*, *Zeek*, and as part of limited-edition chapbooks from Octopus Books and Supermachine. I thank the editors of these publications, especially Ben Fama, Mathias Svalina, and Zachary Schomburg. Deepest gratitude to my family, Sophia and Mikhail Turovsky and Roman Turovsky for their unwavering support; to Ilana Halperin, Tala Hadid, Adam Putnam, Pam Dick, Yasmine Alwan, Jennifer Hayashida, Nadya Nilina, Kio Stark, Carlos Blackburn, Eugene Ostashevsky, Jennifer Carlson, Lisa Benger, Madhu Kaza, Wah-Ming Chang, Anna Moschovakis, and Marie Reagan for their sustained and sustaining conversation and friendship; to Ann Lauterbach for her generosity and creative engagement; to the late Arkadii Dragomoshchenko, whose memory and influence continues to guide me; to Lawrence Hauser, Jessica Benjamin, and Sheila Ronsen, for listening and teaching me to listen. My profound thanks to John Yau and Black Square Editions for shepherding this book into the world. And thank you, ever and always, to Willis Sparks, with love.

ABOUT THE AUTHOR

GENYA TUROVSKAYA was born in Kiev, Ukraine, and has lived most of her life in New York City. She is the author of the chapbooks *Calendar* (Ugly Duckling Presse), *The Tides* (Octopus Books), *New Year's Day* (Octopus Books), and *Dear Jenny* (Supermachine). Her poetry and translations of contemporary Russian poets have appeared in *A Public Space, Asymptote, Chicago Review, Conjunctions, Fence, Gulf Coast, jubilat, Octopus, PEN Poetry, Sangam Poetry, Seedings, The Elephants*, and other publications. She is the primary translator of Aleksandr Skidan's *Red Shifting* (Ugly Duckling Presse) and cotranslator of Elena Fanailova's *The Russian Version* (Ugly Duckling Presse), which won the University of Rochester's Three Percent 2010 award for Best Translated Book of Poetry. She is also a cotranslator of Arkadii Dragomoshchenko's *Endarkenment: Selected Poems* (Wesleyan). She is a practicing psychotherapist and lives in Brooklyn, NY.